Dandelion Child

Palewell Press

Dandelion Child

Selected poems by Frances White

Dandelion Child

First edition 2019 from Palewell Press,
www.palewellpress.co.uk

Printed and bound in the UK

ISBN 978-1-911587-21-7

Acknowledgements

These poems previously appeared in the following Words Poetry Group anthologies -

Away with Words 2007: Dandelion Child, Wall Jumpers, Horse, Ashes, Evening Primroses, Pink Fluff, Piano Bar Blues, Toulouse or not to lose, and Square Park.

A Brush with Words, 2015: Workhorse, Pipe Dreams, Late December, Woman Underground, Tiff, and **Ascension Day in Teddington Churchyard.**

Dedication

Over the course of her life, Frances was part of several wonderful groups of people involved in creative writing and poetry performance. This collection is dedicated to all of you with thanks for your friendly feedback and delight in your shared enjoyment of the written word.

Remembering Frances White

Frances White and I met at Camden Poetry years ago and kept running into each other at poetry events around London. I was delighted when she agreed to do a joint reading with me at Waterstones in Richmond.

She was an active member of Palewell Poets, where I first heard the brilliant sequence of Angel poems featured in this collection. After the success of *Swiftscape*, her first collection, it seemed only a short while before Frances told me and the other Palewell Poets that she had Motor Neurone Disease.

We always tried to attend each other's launches. It was wonderful of her husband, Steve, to bring Frances in her wheelchair to my most recent launch, only last Autumn. Knowing she had a lot of great unpublished work, I offered to bring out a second collection for her.

She talked me through the poems she wanted published – including some she wrote during her illness – and we hoped to work on the collection together but time ran out. Fortunately, Steve really appreciates her poetry and has been an invaluable guide in assembling *Dandelion Child*.

Camilla Reeve, Editor

Contents

SEASONS

Wall Jumpers

"Damned wall jumpers in Top Pasture!"
He'd noted they weren't all his sheep
and went back after supper
to sort them out.
No moon, his boots sunk
as he leant into the lower slopes
behind the farmhouse.

He climbed over gate and stile, calling
"Here Meg".
The collie circled the perimeter, sniffing
for treats of afterbirth. In the silence
new lambs were being born
steaming on the cold hillside
to survive or not
he wouldn't know till dawn
but now
he was tracking trespassers.

No sign, till he reached a sheltered hollow
by the last gate onto open fell
and startled a band of ewes.
They thundered in an avalanche over limestone rocks
the white outcrop just discernible.
He'd missed cornering them and cursed
striding down the slope, shouting for the dog.
"To heel! Come in a hint!"
They bolted this way and that, frantic
to escape the collie, as she darted
through the dark and crouched, panting.

2

Stones tumbled when they breached the wall.
He followed through and set to, rebuilding
securing his boundary with fallen slabs
blocking the way he'd come. He knew
another way back, steeper, more slippery
so pitch black, he couldn't see his feet.

"That was a tricky one, eh Meg?
And a torch would've been a good idea."

A Box of Blue Tits

It's the first week of May

parent birds fly from the hole like buds unfurling
in a flurry of flight they round the house searching out insects,
the garden newly green with bluebells, daffodils, tulips to dead-head
small butterflies flutter among honesty, wallflowers, forget-me-not.

Faint cheeps whisper from the box as I slide out of the side door
to the rubbish bins.
Cautious not to be seen re-entering the box with caterpillars
their heads turn almost 360 degrees checking for predators.

Fox

Fox enters my garden at night
leaps over my fence like a cat
scavenges round the dustbin for food

Next day the garden stinks
A mass of feathers on the lawn
A hole tunnelled under the fence

Fox knows how to enter and exit.

Horse

After an uphill climb, we rest awhile
beneath the cool dark pine,
sweetly shaded leisure time,
wishing this hired horse were mine.

Workhorse

Back in harness,
leather reins jolt at the bit.
I taste metal.

Longing for grass,
I trot through noisy traffic,
ready to bolt,

to jump the gate,
canter the fields and roll
like a colt again.

Crows in the Sycamore

How do I know what you are
crow, raven, jackdaw?
Menacing but beautiful
silhouetted in the high sycamore
against a mild winter sky.

Your raucous voices can't be heard
but outside I know the other birdsong
will pierce the air with joy
while you fill me with dread,
forbidding, self-righteous, judgemental,
excluding songbirds from their rites,
their right to life.

One Lone Sycamore

I watch one magpie on one lone sycamore
fanned out against the grey evening sky
in itself a world for different species

Before builders came, pile drilling,
sycamores spread their branches
a tracery of twigs etched against red sunsets

following the sun and moon
raising our sights through the seasons
a universe for birds and squirrels

Swifts, beaks open on top gear flight
targeted insects swirling in the air above
nourishment for their mass exodus.

The looming poplar fell mysteriously.
A fire at the base of the weeping willow,
screech of chain saw before 6am,

piles of wood chippings where sycamores were.
More profit in paying fines than obeying protection orders;
then tall houses and cramped flats.

One lone sycamore left to pelt out seeds in defiance.

Mountain Mist

We thought clouds were soft shape-shifters
floating in the sky as we spurred our ponies on uphill

towards a white cumulus
nesting in the black branches of a dead tree.

Smaller clouds sailed quickly by, a series of smoke signals
their message lost on us as we raced the hilltop wind

The air cooled and a wall of cloud slapped our faces
distant slag heaps turned from black to grey.

Enveloped in swirling mist, three of us fell into line
my brother's horse in front, its tail just visible.

Fingers chilled and slippery, we loosened our reins
trusting the ponies to plough a steady pace.

We knew the ground well, potholes, rocks, the ridge
but recognised nothing.

When I shouted over my shoulder for my sister to keep up
the murky fog swallowed my voice.

My brother disappeared into the cloud without a sound.

God Forsaken Christmas

Christmas, why do you crucify me?
battered shattered by Yuletide
invitations celebrations expectations

short daylight hours and Advent chores
never-ending Christmas cards
mind-numbing traffic jams

to precincts where receivership
shudders on so many shutters
greed's madness cannot save them.

It's down to mother to provide
warm comfort and the perfect gift
while claustrophobic gluttony

invades the home and brings no rest
flotsam jetsam ripped and torn
I wish I could be castaway

to eat fresh fruit and breath clean air
and bathe myself in Peace on Earth
while Herod sways this fuddled feast.

Christmas Eve

We put up a pine tree, lightly laden
a simple crib, plain as a stable
a hint of incense
and a Christmas candle to light the table.

As night turns crisp and frost sets hard
we hear you coming, under the stars
joking and jolly
with no need for gifts or expensive cards.

Bring your chatter and laughter through
bunches of holly and fir cones too
there's plenty of food
and then we'll sing carols old and new

around the pine tree, lightly laden
a simple crib, plain as a stable
a hint of incense
and a Christmas candle to light the table.

Late December

Muddy fields harden
shadowy trees close ranks
freezing puddles set.

North wind lacerates
gravestones tilt out of kilter
grey church huddles down.

Oak doors clank open
footsteps echo on flagstones
holly decks the font.

Carols from the choir
candles flicker round the crib
warm mugs of mulled wine.

Fallen pine needles
dry tree tossed out, roots askew
dustbin crammed with glitz.

Frost shrivels the land
late afternoon moon rises
the old year closes.

CONNECTIONS

Dandelion Child

Dandelion child
down the back alley
playing with boys
in the dirt and gravel
laughing, shouting
shrieking in the sunshine

safe

between gardens
in quiet shadows
gathering brash
ragged blooms
to fill jam jars
in the kitchen.

Lily white adolescence
clean dresses
shy wonder
at the willowherb
towering where we walked
by the railway track

a lull

before hot summers
the rush of freedom
music in the air
wild flowers in our hair
and then the longing
for red roses.

Evening Primroses

Evening primroses
incandescent
in the moonlight.
Every reason
to stay out late
in my garden
tonight.

Rain

Rain on the garden
Rain on the street
Rain on the cars
Rain on my feet
Refreshing, lovely
Greening the grass
Hushing the heat

Black Umbrella

The heatwave ends so suddenly.
I walk the path in sundress and sandals,
bare shoulders chilled by wind,
toes tingling with the needle rain.

Up goes the black umbrella,
grey sky weighing on its silver spokes,
tilted like a fan against angry tides
surging up The Thames.

A skein of geese fly over
honking out a warning.
Behind the clouds a harvest moon
vies with the mid-August sun

Feet freezing with the sharp rain
bare shoulders rounded by wind
in sundress and sandals I splash
clutching a black umbrella in vain.

Son

You plunge into the water
slender and fit
in the splendour of youth
daring and playful.

I want to capture you
here on my camera
keep you golden and perfect.

If I could, I'd give you feathers
to survive the tides of time
wild wings to beat on turbulence

but you'd fly like Icarus
far too near the sun
and tumble out of grace
in all your glory.

Apple Tree

Nine years since my father
with waning strength pruned the espalier
spread uneasily against our garage wall.

Foundations compromised its roots
knobbly branches strained for light
silver mildew curled its leaves
miniature apples dropped green and hard
lay premature on the lawn.

I kept the tree and tended it
to see its pale pink blossom in the Spring
to watch the blue tits flit from twig to twig
couldn't bear to part with it
                till something in its struggle
showed it was ready to give way.

Now, in that space, Wisteria thrives,
its grave and purple beauty twining in the light
but there's no fruit and birds are scarce
so someone else can take their turn at pruning.

27 July 2018

I sit in the half light of a July garden night,
a full moon to my left and a solar lantern to my right,
two bats flitting on ragged wings

round the trees and border bushes.
Pink hydrangeas and purple flocks
fade into the mystery of undergrowth

details drown in foliage, indistinct, dreamy,
except for the roses, white as snow,
drawing moths with their luminescence.

The moon is hiding behind a rooftop now
nothing really stands still; it is hot and quiet as the night
before your departure several years ago.

First Wedding Anniversary

Warm September sun
shone on your wedding day
a year ago today

Cows lowed at guests
pitching tents in fields around
The True Lovers' Knot

The bride's friends fluttered
fixing flowers in her hair
Grandma's pearl necklace

In the pub garden
the groom laughing with his mates
forgot his shaver

***

They came together
light suit and manly stubble
dress, white with lilacs

Slender and graceful
with vows sincere and sacred
to have and to hold

Family rejoiced
confetti, bubbles, petals
love, hugs, photographs

***

The fun of carving
lavish platters of roast meats
on every table

Speeches filtered through
elderflower and champagne
followed by friends' cakes

Little girls and boys
taken away at bed time
trailing mauve sashes.

***

As evening fell
lanterns lit up in the trees
around the fire pit

Guests sat on hay bales
in the warm glow of friendship
telling family tales

Loud disco music
everyone in the marquee
dancing till midnight

***

And now, one year on
from that blest wedding day
a baby on the way

to bring you delight
as you ring out the Old Year
and ring in the New.

Today I Cried

Rifling through the smocks and tunics
on a clothes rail in John Lewis
a warm tear rolled down my cheek.

Up till then I had sorrowed at my son's prognosis
and for you, a young mother, to be widowed
unbelievably too soon in the future.

I'd need to help you grieve and to move on
but the thought of you finding a new mother-in-law
and the potential loss of you dawned on me too.

A few more tears flowed, letting me feel
how much I loved and would do anything for you
then, wiped away, I chose a blouse and got on with my day.

Lessons for a Two-year-old.

Help me put the daffodils in a vase. They're all still wrapped inside their brown papery buds except for one which is half-out like a golden butterfly emerging from a chrysalis and another which is just showing its tip.

You find it hard to aim the stalks into the water and they fall on the floor so I hand them back to you and we count them in, all fifteen.

Fill the glass with water and place on the windowsill where the sun will shine on them and they'll come out, one by one, and fill this room with a shout of joy.

Watch and enjoy them for a few days and see them change slightly.

By the weekend they'll lose their lively brightness. The first to come out will droop its head and turn thin and dry and papery. Then another will wrinkle and shrivel and maybe by the end of that day they will all lose their strength.

And I will buy you another bunch of slightly different daffodils called Narcissi.

STRANGERS

Silver Star Fish

He chose her for
her perfect body,
delicate brown skin,
honest eyes.

He gave her a child,
a breeze block house
in the mud hut village;

visited her several times a year
bearing gifts from Europe,
the silver star fish
shiny and sharp
on a slithery chain.

She kept it in a casket
given by her grandmother
to her mother.
Careful stitches hinged
the rough woven lid
and made clasps to secure it
with a thread of string.

The casket lined with
a circle of bright purple
crepe paper,
simple, authentic,
the necklace incompatible

Stranger

Where did you come from, before you came here?
Your eyes are so dark, your voice clipped with fear,
as you enter McDonald's for cheap food and drink
from girls in white caps, faces flustered and pink.

You sit by the window with cola and chips,
eking them out, licking salt from your lips,
watching guys meet, mouthing words you can't hear,
preparing for parties with arms full of beer.

You reach for a tabloid strewn on the next table,
looking at pictures with words you're not able
to read and enjoy nor find out what went wrong,
but your head lifts up knowing the sound of a song.

Do you dream of a land where people aren't white,
as car headlights flash past on this cold wintry night?
Pull up your collar, watch how you go.
Where did you come from, where will you go?

Sluice Room

After the shaking of heads and condolences
the sister asked if I'd like to see a priest.
I nodded and the chaplain came.

A nurse laid the baby between my legs,
his head on my pelvis
for the priest to bless him

but when I asked
he said he couldn't baptise
as the baby had already died.

They took the baby from my arms
said I could keep him next to me
in his hospital cradle, that night

gave me a number of sleeping pills.
They hardly did the job,
my mind in such pain and turmoil.

I must have slept for a while
till my bladder woke me
but cot and baby were gone.

They'd indicated a door off the room
if I needed the loo.
Somehow, I lowered myself from the bed
still weak from the brutal birth

but I held onto whatever I could to reach the door.
Between the delivery room and toilet
I found a small sluice room
a mop in the bucket by the toilet door

28

and a see-through cradle
covered with a white cot sheet
abandoned by the waste bin.

In disbelief, I pulled back the sheet
and bent to kiss him.
How dare they wheel him away,

'SHROUD COPY' scribbled in capitals
on a torn scrap of rough paper
pinned to his white nightie,

I guessed to be photographed and identified,
another unwanted stillborn statistic
on their records.

I wheeled him back to the bed
cradled him in my arms
baptised him with my tears.

Woman Underground

This is the tunnel between before and after.
I am debris, blasted from my past,
blinded to a yawning future.

I'm here as a deposit, on hold,
my world in chaos, ripped apart,
and you ask if I feel violated.
You can't see my memories twitch and shrivel,
your heart has not been opened by the blast.

When you write your piece,
make your words brief and grey as shell shock.
Your hands are firm, while mine shake,
your voice is steady, mine dry and cracked.
This news report will make good bedding.

I do not recognise the other shadows, lying here
around the rib cage of this charnel,
this tube to God knows where.

Fur Hat

fur-coiled, discreetly sewn,
domed and gently curved,
placed on the silver curls
of her busy head.

Cold winds blast
on empty streets
but she won't stay in.

The hat fits, soft and snug,
silk lining like a second skin,
familiar and comforting.

Ashes

Those luscious lips gave
kissing scores to eager boys
brave apprentices.
Her fiancé now holds against
his broken heart her ashes.
Remains
Impersonal
outrageously refined
fiery passion extinguished
a s h e s.

South West Trains

I board the train and squeeze into a seat,
before I glance around, assessing if
there's any risk of harm, when people cram
inside as doors slide open and then close.

The train makes noisy headway through the night,
as we the silent workers bow our heads,
to read the news, or stare askance, or pray,
avoiding eye contact at any cost.

So many different nationalities
I can't identify, and all unique,
with histories, so varied, ripe and rich,
I want to hear them speak, and know their tale.

If only for one minute, each could stand
to give a thumb nail sketch, it would transform
a deadly half hour journey into town,
and turn our dormant hearts and minds around.

Tiff

The rush hour
train has been delayed.
A tall man yells
"It's your fault not mine!"

She turns away,
no point arguing
with a madman strutting
down the platform.

She knows he's
way beyond reason,
leaves him to act
out his pantomime

to a crowd
who watch him lose it,
stamping, snarling,
"It's your fault, not mine!"

Train

It's bitter cold. There's been a delay,
a long wait for the train today.

Somebody jumped, the station staff say,
onto the line I'd have travelled today.

Dusty windows make sky more grey
when I board the London train today.

Lads sit together, nothing to say,
drink smells on their breath today.

Headphones on, mobile games to play,
we're silent on the train today.

Slowed by signals, I quietly pray
for the life lost on the track today.

At Waterloo we shuffle away
past a platform - Closed Today.

Hurricane Katrina

Katrina came 'n' went,
taking N'Orleans,
land of carnival and dreams,
blew a hole through its heart,
ripped Rhythm 'n' Blues apart.

The Big Easy
gives off a big stink,
her razzmatazz drowned,
as bodies rot and rock
in waters round the Superdome,
where survivors wait and wait
and wait in vain for rescue,
riffraff, awash with waste,
down in The City That Care Forgot.

Necklaces we caught,
indigo, amber, emerald,
strings of light thrown down
from balconies, still shimmer
with the heat of Mardi Gras,
the beat of feet and laughter of lost souls
who'll never dance again
to music in Bourbon Street
as it pours from every nightclub door,
nor 'tip the band' in bars
where they once sat, so easy.

One by one, I finger
the haunting magic
of each tawdry bead,
tuning in to the muddy swell
of the Mississippi Blues.

36

PERFORMANCE

Floor Spot

The words I prepared
rebound
echoing in my ears.

Doors creak and slam
on a clatter of glasses
hubbub from the bar.

What possessed me
knees shaking
to take the mic.

Two females look up
heads tilted together
laughing quietly.

Hairs on a man's forearm
glisten in the front row
he glances at his watch.

Words like, 'boring', 'clichéd'
swirl around my head
thud at my feet.

Drinkers at the back go quiet
eyes shine out
in the dark

letting
my voice unravel
stranger to stranger.

Piano Bar Blues

Dizzy summer night
quenched with lager

her eyes dreamy
with piano bar blues

moving aside their empty glasses
his arm brushed hers

low lighting and soft cushions
made her head swim

they slipped away
into the moonlight

music fading
as they sauntered back

under the larch trees
along the water

his hands in his pockets
all the way home.

Humming

Humming
The very word is bliss,
summer, bees, thoughtfulness.

Reverie
an altered state of being
humming is a symptom of deep content

but hum in private
indulge alone.
Humming cuts others out
can be irritating!

Pink Fluff

(at The Eel Pie Club)

A bit of pink fluff
tied round
a long blond
pony tail
gold ring
piercing her nose
small tattoo
rose-madder tights
this catwalk flamingo
struts from the gloom
catching the spotlight
through the tobacco smoke
gaudy, gorgeous
pulling the beery gaze
of Rizla guys
old as her Dad.

Rhythm 'n' Blues
thumps out its rumpus
on the makeshift stage.
Everyone moves
swings loose
forgets the day
as the nightclub rocks
'n' the beat holds sway.

41

Ostriches

You're so chic, wear clothes so fine,
in fur and feathers look divine.
Those fluffy fronds float with such grace,
light and white against your face,
stroke your cheek and make you blush,
when you're announced the room is hushed.

But 'ostrich' is an ugly word.
On him, his plumes look so absurd.
How come we wear them with such taste?
So beautiful, the human race.

Toulouse Or Not To Lose

How much longer
till I break free
and become a lady.

I return to this attic
in the small hours
dancing feet bruised
thighs aching from high-kick
and strip off the frills
down to underclothes and flesh
they glimpsed
but never saw the real me.

The bath tub
that's where I'd like to be
as I crawl into an unmade bed
all sweat and perfume
grabbing sleep while he stays out.

It will do for a time
dancer and concubine
till I break free
and become a lady.

Revolución T-Shirt

(27.04.2012, Peacock Theatre WC2 –for Patric)

Ballet Revolución
has come to London town,
with explosive Cuban dancing,
so tonight, that's where we're bound.

I'm smitten by the muscleman,
featured on the flier,
leaping in mid-air
to whet the heart's desire.

In the foyer, young girls tempt us
to buy the merchandise.
A Revolución T-shirt
has really caught my eye.

"Twenty quid! That's far too much,"
my husband starts to rant,
"even if we do have friends
with Che Guevara pants!"

He buys me a mojito
with a potent kick of rum,
then guides me to the stalls
and the rhythm of the drums.

As those hot-blooded dancers
cast their noisy Cuban spell
I forget about the T-shirt…
the underpants, as well.

Cliché

Dainty ballerina
in white gauze spinning
soft shoes springing
Degas plaits swinging.

Pretty pirouette
she hopes they'll adore
luke-warm applause
they've seen it all before.

A curtsey to the judges
she'll never last, they say
at the end of the day
dismissed as a cliché.

Pipe Dreams

At last the builders' vans have gone,
leaving her shaken and alone
with a luxury bathroom, fully tiled,
best chrome fittings, designer style,
stainless steel kitchen, pans and kettle,
a fine display of gleaming metal.

To soothe herself, she
pours peppermint tea
from a porcelain pot
and slips outside to a shaded spot.
She's so thin you can see
through her skin to her dreams – where

she walks barefoot on dusty streets
half-dancing to the reggae beat
in a haze of fabric, fruit and flowers,
plantain cooking on roadside fires,
back to the beach where fishermen sing,
hauling their nets as the catch comes in.

Square Park

Above the square park
tower blocks and window blinds
obscure her view.

In the morning rain
her dog pulls his lead, heading
for the new saplings.

She follows his path
through the flower beds, searching
for broken tulips.

No one can see how
their redness makes her heart dance
each velvet petal

smuggled in pockets
through the iron perimeter
back to the grey flat.

Fiery butterflies
spread out on her windowsill
above the square park.

ANGELS

Ascension Day in Teddington Churchyard

(After Thomas Traherne, 17th century poet)

Holly, box and yew trees shine
where arching beech and spire of pine
thrust strong roots
beneath a sea
of bluebells and forget-me-nots.

Gravestones tilt, with faded names,
concealed by lichen, worn by rain.
They know the dead
aren't really gone,
all earthly things will rise again!

This unlocked place is quiet and near,
an Eden where God's gifts appear,
so lavish,
wonderful and strange,
the very birds sing praises here.

As bonfires smoulder and refine
nature's wealth to smoke and ashes,
sunlight darts
between the leaves,
reveals you – risen, shining, free!

Angel–1

(After a line by Toon Tellegen)

An angel kissed a man.
The man, wiped away
the wet imprint,
scowled and turned
to the open window,
raised a finger at the world.
With a slam he
shut out the wind,
stomped from the house
to his white van,
reversed into the road,
gears crunching,
and roared off
to the building site.

All day he boasted
to his work mates:
I thumped him one.
I slapped her round a bit.
but when they stopped
for coffee or a smoke,
the shape of the kiss
persisted like a sore,
festering on his forehead.
He scratched the place
till it burned
like a brand cauterizing
some pestilence
seething underneath
his woollen hat.

Angel–2

A man woke to hear an angel singing
so he reached from his bed to check
the radio hadn't been on all night.

He ran a shower
but the swoosh of water over his ears
didn't drown the song.

He dried himself and looked in the mirror,
appeared no different but thought
he might be going mad.

He banged his head hard on one side
with the heel of his hand but couldn't shift
the heavenly voice.

He coughed and retched up mucus,
scoffed toast and gulped tea
noisily, as always.

Again he checked the radio, the TV,
the ringtone on his mobile phone.
"I'll flatten the b****** doing this to me!"

Glowering, he grabbed his football scarf,
stormed off to join the gang
for a liquid lunch before the match.

"What's up mate, some tart done yer 'ead in?"
"Somethin' like that, mate."
"Nothin' a few pints won't put right, eh lads?

Soon the angel's tune
was masked by raucous laughter,
lost in the rackety hubbub of the pub.

Later, she was kept at bay
by the crowd roaring
football songs and racist chants.

Outside the stadium, a scuffle.
He threw a few wild punches,
and forgot about the irritating voice.

Men in blue appeared from nowhere,
handcuffed him and lead him away,
swearing and spitting.

He didn't sleep a wink in the cell that night.
The shrill soprano rose to such a pitch
the light bulb high above him shattered

but who was going to believe that?

Angel–3

An angel brushed him with her wing
to let him know she was there.

He'd ignored her presence close behind
till a fan of feathers swept lightly over the nape of his neck,

cooled the air, made him shudder.
He could do without this in the supermarket.

It was starting to snow so he was stocking up on
bacon, sausages, tins of beans, soup, beer.

She persisted so he tried to appease her, adding angel cake,
angel delight, crystallized angelica, to the wire basket.

The check-out assistant examined the cake's layers.
"Pretty colours," she observed. "Got a new girlfriend?"

"Get on with it," he grunted.
She pursed her lips and shook the acid-green angelica.

"Planning to poison someone?"
He scratched his neck, roughly.

"Looks like an allergic rash," she said.
"You'd better get some anti-histamines.

Medicines are on Aisle B."

Angel–4

A man picked up the phone to stop it ringing
but said nothing.
An angel's voice flowed from a distance,
How are you?
He inhaled roughly on a cigarette
gave no reply.
I've been wondering how things are going,
she enunciated brightly,
not reminding him of her messages.

He coughed deliberately into the mouthpiece,
not answering.
Have you had any luck on the work front?
Her words fluttered along the line
but fell on metal studs.
"I don't know what the f*** you want
or what you're f****** talking about,"
he yelled and slammed down the phone.

Angel–5

He drew on a fag in the back yard
blood-stained feathers at his feet

sniffed and listened for fox
no clue in the grisly aftermath

couldn't face clearing it now
maybe after breakfast.

He spent a while staring into the pan
fat spat as he turned sausages

kept an ear cocked for the phone
Radio 5 vied with the extractor

dropped a tea bag into a stained mug
electric kettle surged to the boil.

He pondered the improbability
of a goose or dove landing in his yard

went out again chewing a mouthful
to survey the bloody mess

knocked next door to accuse
the neighbour and curse his cat.

Fists deep in his pockets he strode
unshaven down to the river

lit up again on the footbridge
leaned on the iron railings

watching boats tug at their moorings
the dark wake of a lone swan.

He crossed the bridge
sat for a while on the riverbank

in the swan's quiet presence
before returning slowly

to bag up the remains of a disaster
he'd slept through the night before.

Annunciation

What *do* you want this time?
I beg your pardon...
Me, "with child"!
Are you really so naive?
We haven't even tied the knot, yet.

"Bun in the oven"?
No, no, Joe's in Carpentry.
Business is good,
keeps him busy.
I'm quite content in my study
reading books.

There's been *no* "small mistake".
It's all arranged
and I'm going along with it.
Ridiculous age-gap...but
I'm not looking elsewhere, thank you.

Nor am I taken aback
by this "little surprise", as you call it.
Now run along
and stop being a pest.
Your visit is unwelcome.

"How's my father?"
Poor old thing
would have a fit
if he could hear you.
Whatever do you mean,
would I "fancy a little accident"?

The impudence!
Why don't you go and...
get yourself hitched?
I wasn't born yesterday,
you won't get *me* falling
for all this stuff and nonsense.

Ghost fish

At the top of the stairs
something stirs

across the landing
your room now tidy

aquarium gone
bed made up and empty

a golden light floating
in the air

my heart
rock heavy.

MESSAGES

Time

Time spins fast forward
forcing my course. It cares not
that I call for you.
Time will not relinquish me
nor abandon its purpose.

Arthritis

Ouch!
The
pain
in
my
feet
gnaws
at
my
brain,
heart
trapped
in
between.

Hints of Trouble

By autumn,
hints of trouble that began in January were pulling me down,
with every muscle twitch felt in the night;

the food that went cold waiting for me to chew
as my jaw soon tired;

the meals taking longer to prepare
while I chopped, pureed, made sauces and soup.

By Christmas, climbing the stairs, no upward push came to my legs
and grabbing the banister, arm-by-arm, I pulled myself along.

Recently, I've had to grasp my key in a grip to turn it,
the easy clockwise click proving too strong for thumb and forefinger.

Last week I couldn't undo the buttons of your shirt before ironing
as no force entered my finger tips.

This week I started having to write things down on paper,
my voice often slipping to unintelligible.

Saliva causes extra problems with speaking
as a bubble fills my mouth,

more food seeps from my lips and needs wiping away
while I'm trying to eat

and, at night, there's the frozen weight of my paralysed leg
as the hot water bottle attempts to warm it.

When You Wake One Morning

When you wake one morning and the world is upside down,
the builders have sawn your fences and felled trees to the ground.

Gardens disappear under sheds the size of houses,
you're not sure who lives in them.

Sky is blocked by loft extensions appearing like carbuncles
with bulging eyes to oversee your every move.

excavating basement rooms for more people from abroad
who work long hours in restaurants.

The garage was converted years ago,
cars sit on front drives where lawns and hedges used to grow.

Salt Cave

Salt water has entered the cave I inhabit.
It pools around the rocks that are my floor,
swirls like small oceans around each foothold.
I can taste it on my lips but mustn't drink it.
The tang of it upon my tongue is the reminder I don't need
that life has changed.
Sometimes the waves surge and splash like serpents,
sometimes they lie quiet, let the rainwater in,
softly lashing my cheeks.

The Ghost of My Former Self

The ghost of my former self visits me often
sitting beside me, my Gemini twin,
warm, laughing, chatty
unlike the ghosts children create at Hallowe'en.

I tell her I'm glad we walked through meadows, woods and streams
up mountains
clambering over boulders
risking the grey scree
to lift ourselves above
war, politics, arguments.

She comments on how weak I've grown in the past year,
how strange it is to find me quiet,
me who liked to form and voice opinions,
forcibly silenced.
My ghost knows I can still think,
sometimes write my views.

But it's so slow.
They used to say I was
fast as a ferret down a hole.
I'd like some of that speed now

but with this ghost beside me
I don't fear the end.
She tells me,
I'll be able to visit the quick and the dead.

Chapel

Along the cool corridor
from the school hall
to the marble stairway to the Art room
we passed the half-glazed doors
To the silent chapel
Where the nuns prayed
Early morning
Before the school day
And evenings
when the girls had returned home.

Some passed by
never tempted to look in
Some popped in
To sit on the benches
Before a small altar
In a cool clear space
watching sunlight slant
through arched windows
airy and bright
on cream walls
Kneel on the kneelers
In a plain peaceful place
in the middle of the school

During Lent
6 weeks of daily mass
setting off before daylight
trees dark shapes against grey sky
waiting at the bus stop
for the headlights and noisy engine
of the 321 green double decker

my friend got on a couple of stops later,
we passed the sun printers and Croxley paper mills
crossed the river Gade and canal bridges up hill, down hill,
the morning brightening as we rang the bell
to stop the bus at the convent school

Three tramps always at the convent door,
waiting for the little nun to return after
filling their big enamel mugs with hot tea
We let ourselves into the school through the side door,
went straight to the chapel
Between 10 and 20 nuns in black veils and habits
already praying silently before mass.
Mass always brief and intensely prayerful

We took bacon sandwiches for breakfast in the dining room
the nuns, busy in the kitchen, brought us pots of tea
and we chatted with up to four other girls,
Two pairs of sisters who also came through lent.
One pair came every year to pray for their mother who was sick.
The other pair, motherless, lived with a grandmother who died—
Such unbelievable sadness but they always smiled.

What is this call to prayer, this power that draws us,
cushions us against the barbed wire of existence?

I'm older now and many a raw morning
find myself returning to quiet chapel visits
brief weekday masses
the art of prayer.

Epiphany Notes

The night has passed
The day lies open before us
Your gates continually
Shut neither by day nor by night
No more will the sun give you daylight
Nor moonlight shine upon you
Guide our feet into the way of peace

Committal

Whether we commit your body
to earth, fire or water
may your spirit be free as air
to continue its journey.

Coincidence

so we meet again
all seasons weave together
life's basket of light

FRANCES WHITE - BIOGRAPHY

Frances White grew up near London with strong family ties in South Wales. During her teens she was influenced by the songs of Bob Dylan, and the poems of Dylan Thomas, The Liverpool Poets and Robert Frost.

She was one of the poets in *Words* Poetry Group, founded by the late Aeronwy Thomas, daughter of Dylan Thomas. Together the group published their poems in three anthologies: *Away With Words* 2007, *A Ring of Words* 2012 and *A Brush With Words* 2015. Frances was highly commended in the Torbay Open Poetry Competition 2010. Her first poetry collection, *Swiftscape*, was published by The Seventh Quarry Press, 2016.

As an English teacher, and later as a Teacher of the Deaf, she encouraged creative writing in pupils of all ages and abilities. Before her death in 2018 from Motor Neurone Disease, Frances lived in South West London with her husband, Stephen. They have three sons and three grandchildren.

Stephen will be donating proceeds from the sale of this collection to the MNDA (The Motor Neurone Disease Association). To see how you can support the charity's work to discover a cure for this disease, go to https://www.mndassociation.org/

PALEWELL PRESS

Palewell Press is an independent publisher handling poetry, fiction and non-fiction with a focus on books that foster Justice, Equality and Sustainability. The Editor can be reached on enquiries@palewellpress.co.uk

www.ingramcontent.com/pod-product-compliance
Lightning Source LLC
Chambersburg PA
CBHW071119030426
42336CB00013BA/2142